DEPARTMENT OF COMMERCE

Cuba: Providing Support for the Cuban People

SUMMARY: This rule amends the Export Administration Regulations to create License Exception Support for the Cuban People (SCP) to authorize the export and reexport of certain items to Cuba that are intended to improve the living conditions of the Cuban people; support independent economic activity and strengthen civil society in Cuba; and improve the free flow of information to, from, and among the Cuban people. It also amends existing License Exception Consumer Communications Devices (CCD) by eliminating the donation requirement, thereby authorizing sales of certain communications items to eligible end users in Cuba. Additionally, it amends License Exception Gift Parcels and Humanitarian Donations (GFT) to authorize exports of multiple gift parcels in a single shipment. Lastly, this rule establishes a general policy of approval for exports and reexports to Cuba of items for the environmental protection of U.S. and international air quality, and waters, and coastlines. These actions are among those announced by the President on December 17, 2014, aimed at supporting the ability of the Cuban people to gain greater control over their own lives and determine their country's future.

DATES: This rule is effective [INSERT DATE OF PUBLICATION IN THE FEDERAL REGISTER].

FOR FURTHER INFORMATION CONTACT: Foreign Policy Division, Office of Nonproliferation and Treaty Compliance, Bureau of Industry and Security, Phone: (202) 482-4252.

SUPPLEMENTARY INFORMATION:

Background

The United States maintains a comprehensive embargo on trade with Cuba. Pursuant to that embargo, all items that are subject to the Export Administration Regulations (EAR) require a license for export or reexport to Cuba unless authorized by a license exception. The Bureau of Industry and Security (BIS) administers export and reexport restrictions on Cuba consistent with the goals of that embargo and with relevant law. Accordingly, BIS may issue specific or general authorizations for specific types of transactions that support the goals of United States policy while the embargo remains in effect.

On December 17, 2014, the President announced that the United States is taking historic steps to chart a new course in bilateral relations with Cuba and to further engage and empower the Cuban people. The President explained that these steps build upon actions taken since 2009 that have been aimed at supporting the ability of the Cuban people to gain greater control over their own lives and determine their country's future. Today, the Commerce and Treasury Departments are taking coordinated actions to implement this policy.

The President's announcement necessitates changes to the EAR related to exports and reexports to promote more effectively positive change in Cuba, consistent with U.S. support for the Cuban people and in line with U.S. national security interests. This rule implements those changes by adding license exceptions and revising licensing policy as appropriate.

This rule enables the export and reexport to Cuba of items intended to empower the nascent Cuban private sector by supporting private economic activity. Items include building materials for use by the private sector to construct or renovate privately-owned buildings including privately-owned residences, businesses, places of worship and buildings for private sector social or recreational use; goods for use by private sector entrepreneurs such as auto mechanics, barbers and hairstylists and restaurateurs; and tools and equipment for private sector agricultural activity. It is intended to facilitate Cuban citizens' lower-priced access to certain goods to improve their living standards and gain greater economic independence from the state. It also enables the export and reexport to Cuba of items to further support civil society in Cuba.

Additionally, this rule enables the export to Cuba of certain items intended to contribute to the ability of the Cuban people to communicate with one another and with people in the United States and the rest of the world. Those exports include commercial sales of items for the establishment and upgrade of communications-related systems as well as certain consumer communications devices, related software, applications, and hardware. Such exports are consistent with Department of Commerce authorities including with Section 1705(e) of the Cuban Democracy Act (22 USC 6004(e)), which authorizes export of "[t]elecommunications facilities . . . in such quantity and of such quality as may be necessary to provide efficient and adequate telecommunications services between the United States and Cuba."

This rule also enables more donations to the Cuban people by simplifying the process to export and reexport gift parcels to Cuba. Lastly, this rule establishes licensing policy relating to environmental protection and makes technical and conforming changes to the EAR.

The Department of the Treasury's Office of Foreign Assets Control (OFAC) is also making changes to its regulations to implement the President's December 17, 2014, policy announcement.

Specific Changes Made by This Rule

Creation of License Exception Support for the Cuban People (SCP)

This rule creates a new § 740.21 of the EAR -- License Exception Support for the Cuban People (SCP). Prior to publication of this rule, the export or reexport to Cuba of items now eligible under this new license exception generally required a license from BIS.

To support improved living conditions and support independent economic activity in Cuba, License Exception SCP authorizes the export and reexport of commercially sold or donated:

- Building materials, equipment, and tools for use by the private sector to construct or renovate privately-owned buildings, including privately-owned residences, businesses, places of worship and buildings for private sector social or recreational use;

- Tools and equipment for private sector agricultural activity; and

- Tools, equipment, supplies, and instruments for use by private sector entrepreneurs. Note that this provision will, for example, allow the export of such items to private sector entrepreneurs, such as auto mechanics, barbers and hairstylists and restaurateurs.

Items eligible for export and reexport to Cuba pursuant to this portion of License Exception SCP are limited to those designated as EAR99 (*i.e.*, items subject to the EAR but not specified in any Export Control Classification Number (ECCN)) or controlled on the Commerce Control List (CCL) only for anti-terrorism reasons.

To strengthen civil society in Cuba, License Exception SCP authorizes the export and reexport to Cuba of certain *donated* items for use in scientific, archaeological, cultural, ecological, educational, historic preservation, or sporting activities. The activities may not relate to the development, production, use, operation, installation, maintenance, repair, overhaul or refurbishing of any item enumerated or otherwise described on the United States Munitions List (22 CFR part 121) or on the Commerce Control List (Supplement No. 1 to part 774 of the EAR) unless the only reason for control that applies to that item as set forth in the ECCN that controls that item is anti-terrorism.

Additionally, License Exception SCP authorizes the *temporary* export of certain items by persons departing the United States for their use in scientific, archeological, cultural, ecological, educational, historic preservation, or sporting activities or for their use in their professional research. The activities or research may not relate to the development, production, use, operation, installation, maintenance, repair, overhaul or refurbishing of any item enumerated or otherwise described on the United States Munitions List (22 CFR part 121) or on the Commerce Control List (Supplement No. 1 to part 774 of the EAR) unless the only reason for control that applies to that item as set forth in the ECCN that controls that item is anti-terrorism. The research must be directly related to the traveler's profession, professional background or area of expertise, including area of graduate-level full-time study. Items authorized for temporary export must be returned to the United States within two years unless consumed in Cuba, or the exporter has applied for and obtained, prior to the expiration of the two year period, a license from BIS authorizing the items to remain in Cuba longer than two years.

License Exception SCP also authorizes the export and reexport to Cuba of certain items to human rights organizations, individuals, or non-governmental organizations that promote independent activity intended to strengthen civil society. Items eligible for the civil society portion of License Exception SCP are limited to those designated as EAR99 or items on the CCL for which the only reason for control is anti-terrorism.

To improve the free flow of information to, from, and among the Cuban people, License Exception SCP authorizes the export and reexport to Cuba of certain items for telecommunications, including access to the Internet, use of Internet services, infrastructure creation and upgrades. Lastly, License Exception SCP authorizes the export and reexport to Cuba of certain items for use by news media personnel and U.S. news bureaus engaged in the gathering and dissemination of news to the general public. Items eligible for export and reexport to Cuba pursuant to this portion of the license exception SCP are limited to those designated as EAR99 or controlled on the CCL only for anti-terrorism reasons.

Expansion of License Exception Consumer Communications Devices (CCD)

This rule revises License Exception Consumer Communications Devices (CCD) in § 740.19 of the EAR to remove the donation requirement and update the list of eligible items.

License Exception CCD was created in 2009 at the direction of the President to help enhance the free flow of information to and from Cuba (74 FR 45985, September 8, 2009). This license exception authorizes export and reexport of consumer communications devices (commodities such as computers, communications equipment and related items, including personal computers, mobile phones, televisions, radios and digital cameras) that are widely available for retail purchase and that are commonly used to exchange information and facilitate interpersonal communications, as well as certain telecommunications and information security-related software. Prior to publication of this rule, License Exception CCD authorized the export or reexport only of donated items, which limited the incentive to send these items to Cuba. This rule removes the donation requirement in License Exception CCD, thereby allowing export or reexport of eligible items for commercial sale or donation to eligible recipients in Cuba.

This rule makes several minor technical revisions to some of those paragraphs in order to track more precisely current technical specifications for certain items and to state explicitly that some items must be consumer items to be eligible for this license exception.

This rule revises the references to ECCN 5A992 in CCD paragraphs (b)(5) – monitors, (b)(6) – printers, (b)(7) – modems, (b)(10) – mobile phones and related items, (b)(11) – memory devices, and (b)(12) – information security, to read ECCN 5A992.c. Paragraph .c refers to "commodities" regarding which "BIS has received an encryption registration or that have been classified as mass market encryption commodities in accordance with § 742.15(b) of the EAR." The inclusion of this paragraph more precisely describes the devices listed in those CCD paragraphs that are eligible for this license exception.

This rule adds a reference to ECCN 5A992.c to paragraph (b)(1) because most modern personal computers generally would be classified under that ECCN due to their encryption capability. This rule also removes the reference to 0.02 weighted teraflops from paragraph (b)(1) because virtually all personal computers manufactured currently have a higher adjusted peak performance level than 0.02 weighted teraflops.

This rule adds a reference to ECCN 5A991.b.4 to paragraph (b)(7) because certain modems that are widely used in consumer communications (*e.g.*, DSL and ADSL modems) would be classified under ECCN 5A991.b.4.

This rule revises the reference to ECCN 5D992 to read 5D992.c in CCD paragraphs (b)(12) – information security and (b)(17) – software for items in paragraphs (b)(1) through (b)(16). The inclusion of paragraph .c, which covers "'[s]oftware'" for which "BIS has received an encryption registration or that have been classified as mass market encryption software in accordance with § 742.15(b) of the EAR," more precisely describes the mass market devices listed in those CCD paragraphs that are eligible for this license exception.

The other provisions of the license exception remain unchanged.

Expansion of License Exception Gift Parcels and Humanitarian Donations (GFT)

This rule revises License Exception Gift Parcels and Humanitarian Donations (GFT) in § 740.12 of the EAR to remove the note that excludes from eligibility consolidated shipments of multiple parcels for delivery to individuals residing in a foreign country. Due to this note, parties exporting multiple gift parcels in a single shipment have been required to obtain individual validated licenses. Although the requirement is not limited to Cuba, in recent years BIS has received gift parcel consolidation license applications only for Cuba, which are routinely approved. Individuals who wish to send gift parcels to Cuba have had to search for parties that have received consolidation licenses, resulting in an unintended disincentive to donate eligible items to the Cuban people. Removing the note allows export and reexport of multiple gift parcels in a single shipment pursuant to License Exception GFT. All the other terms and conditions of the license exception remain unchanged.

New Licensing Policy for Environmental Protection.

This rule amends the licensing policy for Cuba in § 746.2 of the EAR to add a general policy of approval for exports and reexports of items necessary for the environmental protection of U.S. and international air quality, waters, and coastlines (including items related to renewable energy or energy efficiency). Because environmental threats are not limited by national borders, circumstances may warrant the export and reexport of certain items to Cuba to protect U.S. national interests or international interests. Although the existing Cuba licensing policy in the EAR includes the flexibility to authorize environmental protection-related transactions, this revision notifies the public of the U.S. policy interest in considering applications for such authorizations.

Technical and Conforming Changes

This rule removes from the EAR General Order No. 4 in Supplement No.1 to Part 736, § 748.8(d), and paragraph (d) of Supplement No. 2 to Part 748. Those three provisions addressed aspects of licenses or license applications for consolidated shipments of gift parcels that individually were eligible for License Exception GFT. Because this rule makes the consolidated shipments eligible for the same license exception that applies to the individual gift parcels, the consolidated shipment licenses and the information in General Order No. 4, § 748.8(d) and Supplement No. 2 to Part 748 paragraph (d) are no longer needed.

Section 746.2(b) addresses licensing policy for Cuba. This rule revises text in § 746.2(b)(2) and (b)(4) to account for transactions that are now eligible for new License Exception SCP.

This rule adds new License Exception SCP to the list of available License Exceptions for Cuba in § 746.2 of the EAR.

Export Administration Act

Although the Export Administration Act expired on August 20, 2001, the President, through Executive Order 13222 of August 17, 2001, 3 CFR, 2001 Comp., p. 783 (2002), as amended by Executive Order 13637 of March 8, 2013, 78 FR 16129 (March 13, 2013), and as extended by the Notice of August 7, 2014, 79 FR 46959 (August 11, 2014), has continued the Export Administration Regulations in effect under the International Emergency Economic Powers Act. BIS continues to carry out the provisions of the Export Administration Act, as appropriate and to the extent permitted by law, pursuant to Executive Order 13222 as amended by Executive Order 13637.

Rulemaking Requirements

1. Executive Orders 13563 and 12866 direct agencies to assess all costs and benefits of available regulatory alternatives and, if regulation is necessary, to select regulatory approaches that maximize net benefits (including potential economic, environmental, public health and safety effects, distributive impacts, and equity). Executive Order 13563 emphasizes the

importance of quantifying both costs and benefits, of reducing costs, of harmonizing rules, and of promoting flexibility. This rule has been designated a "significant regulatory action," although not economically significant, under section 3(f) of Executive Order 12866. Accordingly, the rule has been reviewed by the Office of Management and Budget (OMB).

2. Notwithstanding any other provision of law, no person is required to respond to, nor shall any person be subject to a penalty for failure to comply with, a collection of information subject to the requirements of the Paperwork Reduction Act of 1995 (44 U.S.C. 3501 *et seq.*) (PRA), unless that collection of information displays a currently valid Office of Management and Budget (OMB) control number. This rule involves a collection of information approved under OMB control number 0694-0088 – Simplified Network Application Processing+ System (SNAP+) and the Multipurpose Export License Application, which carries an annual estimated burden of 31,833 hours. BIS believes that this rule will have no material impact on that burden. To the extent that it has any impact, this rule could impact the burden in two ways. First, this rule might reduce the burden because it makes some transactions that would otherwise require a license eligible for a license exception. Second, although this rule does not impose any new license requirements, it creates less restrictive licensing policies (*i.e.*, the policies under which the decision to approve or deny a license application is made) for exports and reexports for environmental protection. These less restrictive policies might increase the number of license applications submitted to BIS because applicants might be more optimistic about obtaining approval. BIS believes that reduction in the number of license applications resulting from increased license exception availability is likely to more than offset any increase in the number of license applications resulting from less restrictive licensing policy because the former involves a large number of small transactions whereas the less restrictive license policy impacts a smaller

number of larger value transactions. Moreover, the benefit to license applicants in the form of greater likelihood of approval justifies any additional burden.

Send comments regarding this burden estimate or any other aspect of this collection of information, including suggestions for reducing the burden, to Jasmeet K. Seehra, Office of Management and Budget, by e-mail at *jseehra@omb.eop.gov* or by fax to (202) 395-7285 and to William Arvin at william.arvin@bis.doc.gov.

3. This rule does not contain policies with Federalism implications as that term is defined under Executive Order 13132.

4. The provisions of the Administrative Procedure Act (5 U.S.C. 553) requiring notice of proposed rulemaking, the opportunity for public participation, and a delay in effective date, are inapplicable because this regulation involves a military or foreign affairs function of the United States (*See* 5 U.S.C. 553(a)(1)). This rule is a part of a foreign policy initiative to change the nature of the relationship between Cuba and the United States announced by the President on December 17, 2014. Delay in implementing of this rule to obtain public comment would undermine the foreign policy objectives that the rule is intended to implement. Further, no other law requires that a notice of proposed rulemaking and an opportunity for public comment be given for this rule. Because a notice of proposed rulemaking and an opportunity for public comment are not required to be given for this rule under 5 U.S.C. 553, or by any other law, the requirements of the Regulatory Flexibility Act (5 U.S.C. 601 et seq.) are not applicable.

List of Subjects

15 CFR Part 736

Exports.

15 CFR Parts 740 and 748

Administrative practice and procedure, Exports, Reporting and recordkeeping requirements.

15 CFR Part 746

Exports, Reporting and recordkeeping requirements.

For the reasons set forth in the preamble, 15 CFR Chapter VII, Subchapter C is amended as follows:

PART 736 – [AMENDED]

1. The authority citation for 15 CFR part 736 continues to read as follows:

Authority: 50 U.S.C. app. 2401 *et seq.*; 50 U.S.C. 1701 *et seq.*; 22 U.S.C. 2151 note; E.O. 12938, 59 FR 59099, 3 CFR, 1994 Comp., p. 950; E.O. 13020, 61 FR 54079, 3 CFR, 1996 Comp., p. 219; E.O. 13026, 61 FR 58767, 3 CFR, 1996 Comp., p. 228; E.O. 13222, 66 FR 44025, 3 CFR, 2001 Comp., p. 783; E.O. 13338, 69 FR 26751, 3 CFR, 2004 Comp., p. 168; Notice of May 7, 2014, 79 FR 26589 (May 9, 2014); Notice of August 7, 2014, 79 FR 46959 (August 11, 2014); Notice of November 7, 2014, 79 FR 67035 (November 12, 2014).

Supplement No. 1 to Part 736 – [Amended]

2. In Supplement No. 1 to Part 736, paragraph (d) General Order No. 4 is removed and reserved.

PART 740 – [AMENDED]

3. The authority citation for 15 CFR Part 740 continues to read as follows:

Authority: 50 U.S.C. app. 2401 *et seq.*; 50 U.S.C. 1701 *et seq.*; 22 U.S.C. 7201 *et seq.*; E.O. 13026, 61 FR 58767, 3 CFR, 1996 Comp., p. 228; E.O. 13222, 66 FR 44025, 3 CFR, 2001 Comp., p. 783; Notice of August 7, 2014, 79 FR 46959 (August 11, 2014).

Section 740.12 – [Amended]

4. Section 740.12 is amended by removing the note to paragraph (a).

5. Section 740.19 is amended by:

a. Revising paragraph (a);

b. Revising paragraph (b);

c. Removing paragraph (c); and

d. Redesignating paragraph (d) as paragraph (c).

The revisions read as follows:

§ 740.19 Consumer Communications Devices (CCD).

(a) *Authorization.* This License Exception authorizes the export or reexport of commodities and software, either sold or donated, as described in paragraph (b) to Cuba subject to the conditions in paragraph (c) of this section. This section does not authorize U.S.-owned or -controlled entities in third countries to engage in reexports of foreign-produced commodities to Cuba for which no license would be issued by the Treasury Department pursuant to 31 CFR 515.559. Cuba is the only eligible destination under this License Exception.

(b) *Eligible Commodities and Software.* Commodities and software eligible for export or reexport under this section are:

(1) Consumer computers designated EAR99 or classified under Export Control Classification Numbers (ECCN) 5A992.c or 4A994.b;

(2) Consumer disk drives and solid state storage equipment classified under ECCN 5A992 or designated EAR99;

(3) Input/output control units (other than industrial controllers designed for chemical processing) designated EAR99;

(4) Graphics accelerators and graphics coprocessors designated EAR99;

(5) Monitors classified under ECCN 5A992.c or designated EAR99;

(6) Printers classified under ECCN 5A992.c or designated EAR99;

(7) Modems classified under ECCNs 5A991.b.2, 5A991.b.4., or 5A992.c or designated EAR99;

(8) Network access controllers and communications channel controllers classified under ECCN 5A991.b.4 or designated EAR99;

(9) Keyboards, mice and similar devices designated EAR99;

(10) Mobile phones, including cellular and satellite telephones, personal digital assistants, and subscriber information module (SIM) cards and similar devices classified under ECCNs 5A992.c or 5A991 or designated EAR99;

(11) Memory devices classified under ECCN 5A992.c or designated EAR99;

(12) Consumer "information security" equipment, "software" (except "encryption source code") and peripherals classified under ECCNs 5A992.c or 5D992.c or designated EAR99;

(13) Digital cameras and memory cards classified under ECCN 5A992 or designated EAR99;

(14) Television and radio receivers classified under ECCN 5A992 or designated EAR99;

(15) Recording devices classified under ECCN 5A992 or designated EAR99;

(16) Batteries, chargers, carrying cases and accessories for the equipment described in this paragraph that are designated EAR99; and

(17) Consumer "software" (except "encryption source code") classified under ECCNs 4D994, 5D991 or 5D992.c or designated EAR99 to be used for equipment described in paragraphs (b)(1) through (b)(16) of this section.

* * * * *

6. Section 740.21 is added to read as follows:

§ 740.21 Support for the Cuban People (SCP).

(a) *Introduction.* This License Exception authorizes certain exports and reexports to Cuba that are intended to support the Cuban people by improving their living conditions and supporting independent economic activity; strengthening civil society in Cuba; and improving the free flow of information to, from, and among the Cuban people.

(b) *Improving living conditions and supporting independent economic activity.* This paragraph authorizes the export or reexport to Cuba of items designated as EAR99, or controlled on the

Commerce Control List (CCL) (Supplement No. 1 to Part 774 of the EAR) only for anti-terrorism reasons (*i.e.*, anti-terrorism must be the only reason for control that applies to the item as set forth in the Export Control Classification Number (ECCN) that controls the item). If any other reason for control applies to the item, it is not authorized for export or reexport by this paragraph. The item may be either for commercial sale or donated. The item must be within one or more of the following categories:

(1) Building materials, equipment, and tools for use by the private sector to construct or renovate *privately-owned* buildings, including privately-owned residences, businesses, places of worship and buildings for private sector social or recreational use;

(2) Tools and equipment for private sector agricultural activity; or

(3) Tools, equipment, supplies, and instruments for use by private sector entrepreneurs.

(c) *Strengthening civil society.* This paragraph authorizes the export or reexport to Cuba of certain items for use in specified activities that can strengthen civil society. The items authorized pursuant this paragraph are limited to those designated as EAR99 or controlled only for anti-terrorism reasons on the CCL (*i.e.*, anti-terrorism must be the only reason for control that applies to the item as set forth in the ECCN that controls the item). If any other reason for control applies to the item, it is not authorized for export or reexport by this paragraph. The export or reexport must be within one or more of the following categories:

(1) The export or reexport to Cuba of *donated* items for use in scientific, archaeological, cultural, ecological, educational, historic preservation, or sporting activities. The activities may not relate to the "development," "production," "use," operation, installation, maintenance, repair,

overhaul or refurbishing of any item enumerated or otherwise described on the United States Munitions List (22 CFR Part 121) or of any item enumerated or otherwise described on the Commerce Control List (Supplement No. 1 to Part 774 of the EAR) unless the only reason for control that applies to that item as set forth in the ECCN that controls that item is anti-terrorism.

(2) The *temporary* export to Cuba of items by persons departing the United States for their use in scientific, archeological, cultural, ecological, educational, historic preservation, or sporting activities, or for their use in the traveler's professional research. The following limitations shall apply:

(i) The research must be directly related to traveler's profession, professional background or area of expertise, including area of graduate-level full-time study.

(ii) The activities or research may not relate to the "development," "production," "use," operation, installation, maintenance, repair, overhaul or refurbishing of any item enumerated or otherwise described on the United States Munitions List (22 CFR Part 121) or of any item enumerated or otherwise described on the Commerce Control List (Supplement No. 1 to Part 774 of the EAR) unless the only reason for control that applies to that item as set forth in the ECCN that controls that item is anti-terrorism.

(iii) Items authorized for temporary export by this paragraph must be returned to the United States within two years of the date of export from the United States unless:

(A) The items are consumed in Cuba; or

(B) The exporter applies for and receives a license from BIS, prior to the expiration of the two year period, authorizing the items to remain in Cuba for longer than two years.

(iv) Paragraph (c)(2) of this section does not authorize exports if, at the time of the export, the exporter has "knowledge" that the item exported will remain in Cuba for more than two years.

(3) The export or reexport to Cuba of items to human rights organizations, individuals or non-governmental organizations that promote independent activity intended to strengthen civil society.

(d) *Improving communications.* This paragraph authorizes the export or reexport to Cuba of certain items intended to improve the free flow of information to, from, and among the Cuban people. The items authorized pursuant to this paragraph are limited to those designated as EAR99 or controlled only for anti-terrorism reasons on the CCL (*i.e.*, anti-terrorism must be the only reason for control that applies to the item as set forth in the ECCN that controls the item). If any other reason for control applies to the item, it is not authorized for export or reexport by this paragraph. The export or reexport must be within one or more of the following categories:

(1) The export or reexport to Cuba of items, either sold or donated, for telecommunications, including access to the Internet, use of Internet services, infrastructure creation and upgrades.

(2) The export or reexport to Cuba of items for use by news media personnel engaged in the gathering and dissemination of news to the general public and who are:

(i) Regularly employed as journalists by a news reporting organization;

(ii) Regularly employed as supporting broadcast or technical personnel;

(iii) Freelance journalists with a record of previous journalistic experience working on a freelance journalistic project; or

(iv) Broadcast or technical personnel with a record of previous broadcast or technical experience who are supporting a freelance journalist working on a freelance journalistic project.

(3) The export or reexport to Cuba of items for use by U.S. news bureaus engaged in the gathering and dissemination of news to the general public.

PART 746 – [AMENDED]

7. The authority citation for 15 CFR part 746 continues to read as follows:

Authority: 50 U.S.C. app. 2401 *et seq.*; 50 U.S.C. 1701 *et seq.*; 22 U.S.C. 287c; Sec 1503, Pub. L. 108-11, 117 Stat. 559; 22 U.S.C. 6004; 22 U.S.C. 7201 *et seq.*; 22 U.S.C. 7210; E.O. 12854, 58 FR 36587, 3 CFR, 1993 Comp., p. 614; E.O. 12918, 59 FR 28205, 3 CFR, 1994 Comp., p. 899; E.O. 13222, 66 FR 44025, 3 CFR, 2001 Comp., p. 783; E.O. 13338, 69 FR 26751, 3 CFR, 2004 Comp., p 168; Presidential Determination 2003-23 of May 7, 2003, 68 FR 26459, May 16, 2003; Presidential Determination 2007-7 of December 7, 2006, 72 FR 1899 (January 16, 2007); Notice of May 7, 2014, 79 FR 26589 (May 9, 2014); Notice of August 7, 2014, 79 FR 46959 (August 11, 2014).

8. Section 746.2 is amended by:

a. Adding a paragraph (a)(1)(xiv);

b. Revising paragraph (b)(2);

c, Revising paragraph (b)(4)(i);

d. Revising paragraph (b)(4)(ii); and

e. Adding a paragraph (b)(6) to read as follows:

§ 746.2 Cuba.

(a) * * *

(1) * * *

(xiv) License Exception Support for the Cuban People (SCP) (*see* § 740.21 of the EAR).

* * * * *

(b) * * *

(2) Telecommunications items may be authorized for export or reexport to Cuba on a case-by-case basis.

* * * * *

(4) * * *

(i) Applications for licenses for exports of certain commodities and software may be approved to human rights organizations, or to individuals and non-governmental organizations that promote independent activity intended to strengthen civil society in Cuba when such exports do not give rise to U.S. national security or counter-terrorism concerns. Applicants may donate or sell the commodities or software to be exported. Reexport to other end-users or end-uses is not authorized.

(ii) Commodities and software may be approved for export to U.S. news bureaus in Cuba whose primary purpose is the gathering and dissemination of news to the general public.

*****

(6) Applications for exports or reexports of items necessary for the environmental protection of U.S. and international air quality, waters, or coastlines (including items related to renewable energy or energy efficiency) will generally be approved.

* * * * *

PART 748 – [AMENDED]

7. The authority citation for 15 CFR part 748 continues to read as follows:

Authority: 50 U.S.C. app. 2401 *et seq.*; 50 U.S.C. 1701 *et seq.*; E.O. 13026, 61 FR 58767, 3 CFR, 1996 Comp., p. 228; E.O. 13222, 66 FR 44025, 3 CFR, 2001 Comp., p. 783; Notice of August 7, 2014, 79 FR 46959 (August 11, 2014).

Section 748.8 – [Amended]

8. In §748.8, remove and reserve paragraph (d).

Supplement No. 2 to Part 748 – [Amended]

9. In Supplement No. 2 to part 748, remove and reserve paragraph (d).

Dated: January 12, 2015

Penny Pritzker,

Secretary of Commerce.

[FR Doc. 2015-00590 Filed 01/15/2015 at 8:45 am; Publication Date: 01/16/2015]